A Busy Beaver

by Michael Falcon

HOUGHTON MIFFLIN HARCOURT
School Publishers

PHOTOGRAPHY CREDITS: Cover Yva Momatiuk/John Eastcott/Minden Pictures. 1 Yva Momatiuk/John Eastcott/Minden Pictures. 2 © stanley45/iStockPhoto.com. 3 © jeeper/iStockPhoto.com 4 M. A. Battilana/Alamy. 5 Matthew Johnston/Alamy. 6 Yva Momatiuk/John Eastcott/Minden Pictures. 7 © smileitsmccheeze/iStockPhoto.com. 8 Ace Stock Limited/Alamy. 9 M. A. Battilana/Alamy. 10 Jerry and Marcy Monkman/EcoPhotography.com/Alamy.

Printed in China

ISBN-13: 978-0-547-02566-7
ISBN-10: 0-547-02566-1

15 16 17 18 0940 20 19 18 17
4500634148

Beaver

Look at this beaver.
It is cutting a tree down
with its teeth.
It will build a dam.

Dam

The dam will stop the water in a stream and make a pond.
A beaver uses mud and branches to build its dam.

Swimming

A beaver lives in a pond because
the deep water keeps it safe.
Most animals that like to eat
beavers are not good swimmers.
They can't hunt the beavers
in the water.

Beaver home

A beaver builds its home
in the pond made by its dam.
It builds a round home of mud
and branches.
A beaver has to swim under the
water to get into its home.

5

Branch

A beaver eats plants that grow
in the pond.
It also eats leaves and bark on the
trees that grow around the pond.
A beaver uses its sharp teeth
to cut off branches.
In the fall, it puts branches
in the pond so it can eat them
in the winter.

Beaver tail

A beaver uses its tail to warn others
when an enemy comes too close.
A beaver will slap its tail
on the water.
The tail's flat shape makes
a loud smack!
That slap says "Danger!"
to other beavers.

Broken dam

Sometimes the stream will flood
and break the beaver's dam.
Then the pond disappears!
The beaver must get to work
and build its dam again.

Baby beaver

Baby beavers are born in the pond.
A beaver leaves the pond when it is
two years old.
Then the young beaver works
hard, too!
It builds a new dam and makes
a new pond.

Beaver pond

If you spend time at a beaver pond,
you will know why a beaver is
so busy.
You will see the beaver's amazing
home and dam.

Responding

Text and Graphic Features What do the photos in this book show you? Look back at the pictures in the book. Copy the chart below. Fill in what you learned.

Photos	Page	What They Show
Beaver ?	2 ?	Chewing a tree ?

✏ Write About It

Text to World Write a few sentences that summarize why beavers are so busy. Use some ideas from the chart above. Remember that a summary tells the most important ideas in just a few sentences.

✔ **TARGET SKILL** **Text and Graphic Features** Tell how words go with photos.

✔ **TARGET STRATEGY** **Question** Ask questions about what you are reading.

GENRE **Informational text** gives facts about a topic.